Clifton Park - Halfmoon Library

W9-AYQ-963

Let's Read About Our Bodies

Nose

By Cynthia Klingel and Robert B. Noyed

Reading consultant: Cecilia Minden-Cupp, Ph.D.,
Adjunct Professor, College of Continuing and Professional Studies, University of Virginia

Gareth Stevens
Publishing

Clifton Park - Halfmoon Public Libra
475 Moe Road
Clifton Park, New York 12065

Please visit our Web site www.garethstevens.com. For a free color catalog of all our high-quality books, call toll free 1-800-542-2595 or fax 1-877-542-2596.

Library of Congress Cataloging-in-Publication Data

Klingel, Cynthia.
    Nose / by Cynthia Klingel and Robert B. Noyed.
      p. cm. — (Let's read about our bodies)
    Includes bibliographical references and index.
    Summary: An introduction to the nose, what it is used for, and how to take care of it.
    ISBN: 978-1-4339-3371-4 (lib. bdg.)
    ISBN: 978-1-4339-3372-1 (pbk.)
    ISBN: 978-1-4339-3373-8
    1. Nose—Juvenile literature. [1. Nose. 2. Smell. 3. Senses and sensation.]
  I. Noyed, Robert B. II. Title.
  QP458.K553 2002
  611'.21—dc21
3747
2001055054

New edition published 2010 by
Gareth Stevens Publishing
111 East 14th Street, Suite 349
New York, NY 10003

New text and images this edition copyright © 2010 Gareth Stevens Publishing

Original edition published 2003 by Weekly Reader® Books
An imprint of Gareth Stevens Publishing
Original edition text and images copyright © 2003 Gareth Stevens Publishing

Art direction: Haley Harasymiw, Tammy Gruenewald
Page layout: Daniel Hosek, Katherine A. Goedheer
Editorial direction: Kerri O'Donnell, Diane Laska Swanke

Photo credits: Cover © Paul Bradbury/Getty Images; pp. 5, 9, 11, 13, 15, 17, 19, 21 Gregg Andersen; p. 7 shutterstock.com.

All rights reserved. No part of this book may be reproduced in any form without permission in writing from the publisher, except by a reviewer.

Printed in the United States of America

CPSIA compliance information: Batch #WW10GS: For further information contact Gareth Stevens, New York, New York at 1-800-542-2595.

Table of Contents

Boldface words appear in the glossary.

My Nose

This is my nose.
I can touch
my nose.

5

So Many Smells

I use my nose
to smell things.

Some things smell good.

Some things smell bad!

Breathe Deep!

I use my nose to breathe.

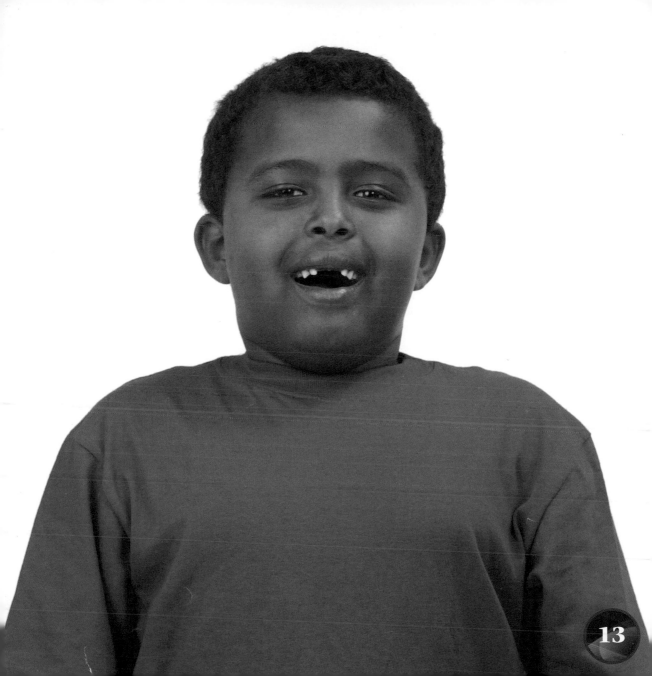

Some things make my nose itch. Pepper and dust make me **sneeze**.

Sometimes my nose feels **stuffy**.

Caring for Noses

Sometimes my nose is runny. Then I have to wipe my nose.

I take good care of my nose. I wear a **mask** when I play sports.

Glossary

breathe: to take air into the lungs and then let it out

mask: a covering that protects your face

sneeze: air that is suddenly forced from the nose and mouth

stuffy: closed up

For More Information

Books

Boothroyd, Jennifer. *What Is Smell?* Minneapolis, MN: Lerner
  Publishing Group, 2010.

Douglas, Lloyd G. *My Nose.* New York: Children's Press,
  2004.

Perkins, Al. *The Nose Book.* New York: Random House Books
  for Young Readers, 2002.

Randolph, Joanne. *Whose Nose Is This?* New York: PowerKids
  Press, 2008.

Slater, Michael David. *Ned's Nose Is Running!* Minneapolis,
  MN: Magic Wagon, 2009.

Web Sites

Your Nose

kidshealth.org/kid/htbw/nose.html

For information about the different parts of the nose

Publisher's note to educators and parents: Our editors have carefully reviewed these Web sites to ensure that they are suitable for students. Many Web sites change frequently, however, and we cannot guarantee that a site's future contents will continue to meet our high standards of quality and educational value. Be advised that students should be closely supervised whenever they access the Internet.

Index

About the Authors

Cynthia Klingel has worked as a high school English teacher and an elementary school teacher. She is currently the curriculum director for a Minnesota school district. Cynthia Klingel lives with her family in Mankato, Minnesota.

Robert B. Noyed started his career as a newspaper reporter. Since then, he has worked in school communications and public relations at the state and national level. Robert B. Noyed lives with his family in Brooklyn Center, Minnesota.